Pigs
Wild and Tame

Pigs
Wild and Tame

by Alice L. Hopf

HOLIDAY HOUSE · *New York*

For my husband Ernest

Library of Congress Cataloging in Publication Data

Hopf, Alice Lightner, 1904–
  Pigs wild and tame.

  Includes index.
  SUMMARY: Introduces the domestic pig and a variety
of wild ones including the wild boar, bushpig, pigmy
hog, warthog, and peccary.
  1. Suidae—Juvenile literature. [1. Suidae.
2. Pigs] I. Title.
QL737.U58H66   599'.734   79-2110
ISBN 0-8234-0364-5

Contents

The pig family has played a part in human civilization for a long time. This is a relief sculpture of a wild boar from ancient Persia (now Iran).

1 · The Pig Has Been with Us a Long Time

Pigs have been rooting about our planet for some 40 million years, and there has been remarkably little change in them during that time. While other hoofed mammals grew larger or smaller, and developed specialized teeth or extra stomachs to deal with the new grasses that appeared later in their evolutionary life, the pigs continued their habit of eating almost anything and required little change in their physical makeup.

Farmers have raised pigs among their barnyard animals for many thousands of years. Just precisely when and where the pig was first domesticated is still a matter of dispute, but the bones of domesticated pigs have turned up in excavations of the dwellings of early humans, beginning with the later part of the Neolithic period, or New Stone Age. This is the time, anywhere between 3000 and 8000 B.C., when people began to give up their wandering and hunting life and settled down to raising crops and living in small communities.

In earlier periods, humans had domesticated the dog (from the wolf) to help them in hunting. Later, when some peoples became nomads, following the herds of reindeer and other animals, the dog was helpful in herding these beasts. And in the nomadic periods, animals like goats and cattle were domesticated, because they are easily herded and persuaded to follow the paths the nomads were taking.

But the pig is a more stubborn and individualistic creature. It insists on going its own way and is not easily herded on long journeys. For this reason, it was not until people settled down to raising grain and other crops and became the first farmers that they began to appreciate the domestic potential of the pig.

Symbiosis with People

Some people may think that the first farmers looked around for a good animal to keep in the barnyard and decided on the pig. But Frederick E. Zeuner, an expert on domesticated animals, believes that all domestication was a gradual process, and in a sense biological. It is a kind of symbiosis: a living together of two quite different species. In some cases symbiosis is a relationship that is beneficial to both of them; in other cases this is not so. With the dog, domestication began in the hunting period, when wolves would come around human camps looking for bits of meat and bones that might have been left by the hunters. Some more kind-hearted hunters—or perhaps merely experimental—took to throwing tidbits to the wolves and thus some animals were lured into staying near the human camps and taking part in the hunts.

Zeuner points out that in most cases of symbiosis, one species has the better of the deal. These biological relationships have often occurred in nature before human domestication of animals began. They can be seen among the ants, where many other creatures share the ants' nest. Beetles, caterpillars, and spiders are all known to make homes with ants. Sometimes this is benefical to the ants, which suck up a sweet nectar exuded by their guests. But often it is really harmful to the owners of the nest, for the guests may eat their eggs and larvae.

Zeuner mentions one unusual case in which symbiosis is mutually beneficial. Two different species of ants, one large (*Camponotus femoratus*) and one small (*Crematogaster parabiotica*) build their nests together in a kind of ball around the branch of a tree. The little ants live in the outer part of the nest and the big ones live deep inside. Their corridors intersect one another and the two species go out foraging to-

This Landrace gilt pig is most people's idea of a "porker" that produces meat products for human use. It is only one of many breeds, however. "Landrace" means that it is a Danish bacontype hog, and "gilt" usually means a female that has not yet produced a first litter.

gether. If the nest is disturbed only slightly, the little ants run out in defense. But if the branch is shaken violently, the big ants come rushing out to attack. Neither species has a better position in the relationship than the other.

This is far from the case in our domestication of animals. The animal finds a safe haven with people. It is protected from its enemies and given a good supply of food. But in return it becomes a slave to its master. It supplies help in hunting or herding, works hard as a beast of burden, and gives up its life to feed the humans who support it. This last is especially true of the pig. While its skin and other parts of its body are very useful for making articles of clothing and other items, it is the tender, tasty meat that has made this animal so popular around the world.

We can imagine the wild pigs of that early Stone Age period, invading the simple gardens and rooting about in the garbage piles. The farmers would hasten to defend their plantings, and the pigs that were killed in the fracas would have added a tasty and nourishing meal to the farmer's menu. But pigs are not easily frightened away from food, and the groups of wild boars must have returned regularly to the beckoning food supply. This symbiotic relationship may have continued for many years before it occurred to some farmers that it was easier to kill the pigs on the home ground than to go hunting for them in the forest. And so the pig was taken into the farmyard, fed and fenced away from the garden plot and butchered on the spot when the time came to eat it.

The Two Biggest Toes

The pig is a hoofed animal, an ungulate, and belongs to that large group that scientists call the even-toed ungulates (Artiodactyla). People speak of these animals—which include cattle, deer, goats, sheep, and camels—as cloven-hoofed. But rather than having a split hoof, they have retained the two largest toes—

the second and third of the original five—to run on. The weight of the animal comes down between these two toes, which have grown into hoofs, while the other toes have atrophied, or weakened and stopped developing, and in some cases disappeared. All these animals are quite different from the horse and its few relatives, where the weight is placed on the one middle toe. The horse and its relatives are known as uneven-toed ungulates (Perissodactyla), because with these animals the middle toe has become the solid hoof, while the other toes have disappeared during the millennia of evolution. For some reason, the uneven-toed ungulates have not been as successful in the struggle for life, and only a few species remain of the many that once inhabited the earth. There are many more varied species of the even-toed ungulates still to be found around the world.

Perhaps one reason is that most of the even-toed ungulates have developed complicated digestive systems, with several stomachs. Such animals are known as ruminants. They quickly fill their first stomach (rumen) with food and then retire to a safe and sheltered place where they rest while they regurgitate the food and chew it over again, after which it goes down into the second and third and perhaps even fourth stomachs for digestion. This is known as chewing the cud, and all animals that do that are called ruminants. Some scientists believe that this habit of the ruminants has given them an edge in survival over the horse, which must do all its eating out in the open, a prey to its enemies.

The pig, however, is the most primitive of the even-toed ungulates. It did not develop a complicated set of stomachs, like the ruminants. But it has not been almost harried out of existence, as has the horse. Perhaps one reason is that the pig is a fighter. It has a set of knifelike tusks and a lethal bite, and it often turns on its enemies and fights rather than seeking safety in flight. Even today, the domestic pig is considered a risky animal to tackle in an unfriendly manner.

Knowledge from Garbage Piles

Scientists who spend their lives digging into the past find many animal bones in kitchen middens, or garbage piles left by ancient peoples. The big problem is to decide whether the bones belong to wild or domestic animals. The process of domestication and the gradual breeding of the animals to fit the needs of the farmer bring many changes in the animal, and these can be seen in the bones. An expert can thus decide whether the bones belonged to a wild or domestic beast, and this gives a clue to the kind of culture of the people who left the bones behind. If the animal was wild, it was killed in a hunt and the people who killed and ate it were chiefly hunters. But if it was domesticated, the people had taken on more settled ways. If it was a goat or a reindeer, they may have been nomadic, following their herds for certain periods of the year. But if there are bones of domestic pigs in the middens, the people were in all probability settled farmers.

During the 1860s, the water level of certain lakes in Switzerland fell to a new low and exposed the remains of prehistoric villages. Over a hundred sites were excavated and the ruins were found to date to 6000 and 7000 B.C. The villages had been built upon poles and platforms out in the lakes and the investigators found many relics of the Neolithic, late Stone Age culture. Among the bones of animals were those of the pig. Hogs, goats, and cattle were kept in sheds out on these platforms, where people and animals were safe from marauding enemies. Sometimes the animals were even kept in the houses.

Among these bones, scientists found those of a small, delicately built pig, perhaps more suitable for keeping in a platform shed, or even in a house. This has led to considerable argument, for the European wild hog is a large, heavy animal. Were these little pigs (called turbary pigs) bred from the larger wild boar (*Sus scrofa*) or were they imported from somewhere else? Today the domestic pigs of China are smaller than our domestic pigs, which owe their

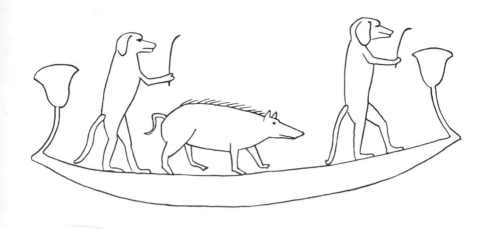

This early illustration is from an ancient Egyptian sarcopha-gus, or stone coffin. It shows a domesticated pig—much re-sembling the medieval European pig—on a boat, guarded by two monkeys.

origin to the European wild hog. But Chinese pigs have often been imported to breed with our pigs, so that there is obviously a close relationship between these strains.

In China, early Neolithic excavations date from 5000 B.C., and in some of them the bones of domestic pigs have been discovered. It is thought that in China proper, nomadic cultures did not develop. The early peoples went from hunting into a settled way of life, and the pig was quickly domesticated. A small pig can be raised right in the house along with the family. Even in China today, the chief domestic animals are the dog, pig, and chicken.

There are other early excavations that also show the

domestic pig. At Anau, in Soviet Turkestan, there is evidence of the pig as far back as 3468 B.C. And in ancient Sumer, the civilization in Mesopotamia that preceded the Egyptian, 18 finds of domestic pigs have been made. Scientists have even found a clay tablet which was a bill for alcoholic beverages, flour, and pork, all eaten at a holiday festival. In Egypt, little clay pigs were buried with the dead before 3400 B.C.

It would seem that as soon as people developed into farmers, they began to realize the importance of the pig as a domestic animal. But whether this happened in one area and then spread to others, or was done at the same time in several places, cannot be answered positively. Wild pigs are native to most parts of the world where humans have lived, so the process of domestication could have happened many times. We will probably never know whether the people of those ancient Swiss Lakes got their pigs from the forests around them or imported them from the Near East or even from as far away as China.

In the ancient world, the pig was valued for both food and other uses. The Romans developed pork into a complicated gourmet cuisine. And herded pigs were a help in the spreading development of farmlands. Their rooting in the ground turned up the soil and their habit of eating roots, shoots, and seeds of all kinds helped clear the forest of undergrowth and prepare the way for fields and farmlands. Moreover, pigs can be pastured on all kinds of wasteland, for they will eat almost anything. They are not strict vegetarians, like the ruminants, but will eat grubs, worms, insects, and even snakes. In fact, they like meat as much as we do. Nuts and fruit, mice, and other rodents are also part of their diet.

Pigs as Workers and Performers

The pig was so popular as a source of food that only occasionally has it been used for other purposes. But it seems to have a much larger potential than most people realize. The ancient Egyptians used the pig to help in their planting. Their little hoofs made holes of just the right size and depth for the seeds, and the animals were driven back and forth over the land to be planted. This was called "treading the seed." They were also used for threshing, being made to walk upon the garnered grain and thus separate the wheat from the chaff.

Later peoples have found other useful work for pigs to do. In medieval England there were strict laws against hunting. The deer were considered the property of the lord who ruled the area and peasants were forbidden to hunt anything except small game. For this reason they could not keep large dogs. Dogs small enough to creep through an iron stirrup, 10½ by 7½ inches, were considered too small for hunting.

A pig hunting out truffles by smell, in Périgord, France. Notice the collar and leash, which help to prevent the animal from eating the valuable truffles itself.

But any dog of a larger size was banned. If the peasant wished to keep such a dog, it would have to be crippled by having some toes cut off.

In this situation the English peasants developed the pig as a hunting companion. Pigs have a keen sense of smell and they are highly intelligent animals —some say more intelligent than the dog. And so in medieval England they were used to lead the poor hunter to forbidden game. Naturally, few records of these illicit activities have come down to us. But there is a detailed record of a remarkable nineteenth-century pig and even an oil painting of her. This pig, named Slut, belonged to Sir Henry Mildmay, and began acting as a retriever when she was 18 months old. Her nose was said to be better than that of any hunting dog Sir Henry ever owned, and she pointed out partridges, pheasants, snipe, and rabbits. When Sir Henry called her to go hunting, she would come running and act as enthusiastic as any dog.

Another use of pigs that is practiced even today in France is that of looking for truffles. These are a kind of black fungus which grow underground, anywhere from two to 12 inches deep. They are highly prized in France as a great delicacy, and as they are rare, and getting rarer, they bring a high price—as much as $200 per pound. Pigs, which are natural rooters and grubbers, are also fond of truffles, and in southwestern France they have been trained to smell out this treasure. Usually the pig has a ring around its snout to keep it from eating the truffles before the collector can grab them and put them in the basket.

Pigs have been trained as circus animals. In fact, one trainer says that they learn more quickly and remember longer than do dogs. As long ago as the fifteenth century, the French king Louis XI delighted in watching a troupe of dancing pigs. And they still can make a popular circus act. The only problem is that pigs grow to be so big and heavy that when they reach a certain age and size they must be retired and a new act trained to replace them. However, a small strain of pigs has recently been developed, primarily for use in the laboratory. In all probability, circus people will soon find a use for them too. Pigs can do anything that dogs can do: jump through hoops, dance, pull a cart, and walk a tightrope. They can also do things a dog would not figure out, like how to open the bolt on a door.

With so many accomplishments, one would think the pig might be an honored member of the farmyard. But although pork is very popular on the table, the pig itself has suffered from a bad press. To call another person a pig is a grave insult in almost every language, and our popular language is full of expressions like "dirty as a pig," "greedy as a pig," and just plain "Don't be a pig." All of this is more an insult to the pig than to the person, for pigs are not by their own nature dirty. It is when a domestic pig is shut up in a garbage-strewn pigsty that it becomes dirty. And a pig is no greedier than any other animal. In fact, it knows when it has eaten enough better than the horse or the dog or cat. All these animals will overeat—but not the pig. If it roots around in its trough, sometimes throwing the food about, it is to find the morsels it especially likes, rather than simply eating everything in sight. And the pig is a good-natured animal. This

When pigs are treated gently they are good-natured animals, though they have an independent spirit. These piglets are from a miniature breed. USDA

does not mean it is subservient. It refuses to be "pushed around," and if treated badly it will react accordingly. But if it is treated with gentleness, it will do almost anything that is asked of it.

Taboos and Diseases

Still, there are many people who do not like pigs, and a number of sects that will not even eat its tender meat. Scientists have argued about the origins of the strong taboos against eating pork, held by such peoples as the Jews and Moslems. These must have originated in the distant past, when such people lived a nomadic life. Nomads do not include pigs among their domestic animals, and nomads are proud, free people who look down on and despise the settled life style of farmers and others who live in communities. Feeling superior to the farmers, they also scorned the farmers' animals and disdained the meat that the farmers ate.

But there may be also a more practical reason behind the taboos on pork. Pigs are very close to humans in their physical makeup and they are prone to a number of serious diseases and parasites which can be passed on to people when their flesh is eaten. One of these is trichinosis.

The disease is caused by the trichina worm (*Trichinella spiralis*), a microscopic roundworm that is often

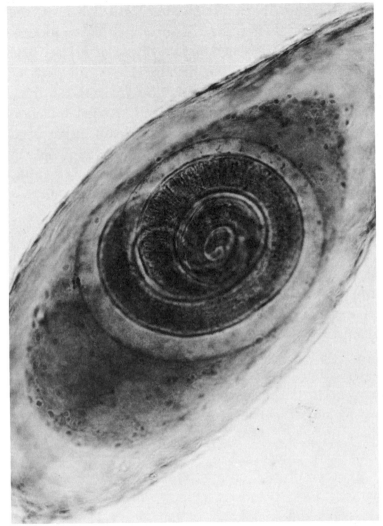

Trichinella spiralis, *the worm that causes trichinosis, encysted in muscle.*

found in pigs. If people eat such infected meat, the worms enter their digestive systems and reproduce, liberating hundreds of young worms, or larvae. The larvae are carried by the bloodstream to all parts of the body. A trichinosis infection begins with diarrhea, nausea, and severe muscular pains. A bad infection can cause fever, delirium, and even death. It has been estimated that as many as 20 per cent of the people in the United States are infected with trichina worms. This amounts to some 40 million Americans suffering from this important parasite.

It is no wonder that certain peoples, noting this serious disease that can come from eating the meat of pigs, have declared them to be unclean and established laws against using pork for food. But there is an easy and simple method of protecting oneself against the trichina worm, and that is to be sure that any pork one eats has been well cooked in a very hot oven. High heat is sufficient to kill any worms that may be in the meat. But of course it is also best to try to keep the live pigs free of worms by feeding them on good, clean food, and not on garbage that may carry parasites.

Another disease of pigs that is also caused by a parasite is cysticercosis (tapeworm disease). There are many different kinds of tapeworms. Some infest beef and some fish, but the pork tapeworm (Taenia) becomes mature in humans, where it reproduces and lays its eggs. Tapeworms have long, flat bodies and the head is provided with hooks or suckers with which it attaches itself to the intestines of its host. There it absorbs the digested food through its body. Many tapeworms are hermaphroditic, having both male and female organs. Again, the way to avoid contracting pork tapeworms is to be sure that all pork products are well cooked. The same rule applies to beef and fish; people who eat raw fish are definitely taking a chance. Certain tapeworms occur sometimes in dogs; their eggs may reach our stomachs and cause trouble.

A third disease that may come from eating pork is undulant fever (brucellosis). It is caused by bacteria (*Brucella suis*). The symptoms are chills and fever, aches, pains, and weakness. Sometimes the symptoms are similar to those of meningitis, or brain fever, and an attack can leave the patient with arthritis or neuritis. Today this disease can be treated with antibiotics. Undulant fever is also carried by cattle and goats and can be contracted by drinking their milk or eating the meat. An effective vaccine has been developed for cattle, but so far such efforts have been unsuccessful with pigs and goats.

Their Breeds Are Many

Over the centuries, the domestic pig, descended chiefly from *Sus scrofa*, has been raised all around the

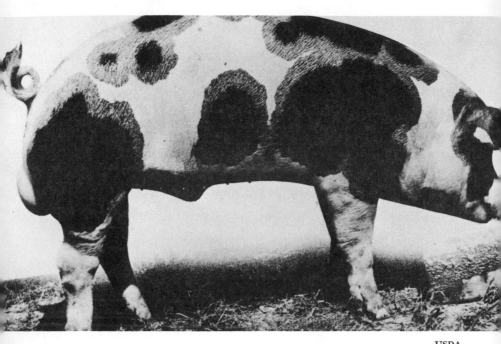

One of the many pig types developed by American farmers is the spotted swine.

world, and many different breeds have resulted from the efforts of people to make a perfect pig for their particular needs. One of the changes that have come with domestication is in color. White is not often seen in nature, for if an albino does occur, it seldom survives. It is more easily caught by predators and usually is shunned by others of its kind. But white is often bred into domestic stock, and in the case of hogs, there are several breeds of pure white animals. Similarly, pied, or mottled, coloring is unusual in nature, with the exception of infants, where a splotched coloring is good camouflage. But most adult wild animals have a solid color. One of the exceptions is the African wild dog, which boasts vivid splotches of color all over its body, each individual showing a different pattern. Domestic pigs, like some horses, have been bred with spots and mottled coloration as well as various patterns of black and white.

American pigs were largely imported from England with some help from the continent; and with skilled breeding techniques we developed our own breeds.

The Hampshire is a handsome white-belted animal. USDA.

In this century, attention has been focused on breeding pigs that will reproduce faster, have larger litters and grow to maturity sooner, at the same time producing more muscle and fat.

In 1823, a breed called the Berkshire was imported from England to America. This pig is black with white feet and a white stripe on face and tail tip. We also developed a breed called the Landrace from Danish stock brought over in 1934. And a breed called the Poland China was developed in Ohio as long ago as 1800. In Indiana, farmers went in for spotted pigs, bred from the Poland China and a breed called Gloucester Old Spots. All-white breeds include the Chester White (from Pennsylvania) and the Yorkshire, which originated in England. All-white pigs, if put out to pasture, may get sunburned. Among the darker breeds are the Duroc-Jersey, which is reddish in color, varying from light to almost dark brown, and the Hampshire, a black pig with a white belt around its body that also covers both front feet.

All these breeds have their good and their undesirable points. Some may be more prolific than others, or the sows may be better mothers and less inclined to lie on their many progeny. Some may produce better meat. If the pigs are to be put out on the rough ground of pasture for some of their food, they should have strong legs and hindquarters; but if they are to be raised in a barn or sty, that consideration is not so important.

Undoubtedly, the domestic pig has come a long way from its natural wild state, just as with other domesticated animals. But it has kept its basic qualities of independence, curiosity, and courage—as well as intelligence—which have allowed it to survive for millions of years in the wild.

2 · The Formidable Wild Boar

The wild boars of the genus Sus are the most widely distributed of all the pig family, and of these *Sus scrofa*, the wild boar of Europe, has the largest range. (Its common name, male and female, is "wild boar," but it should be noted that the word "boar" is often used for only the male of any pig species.) It is found in Europe and Asia, as well as in North Africa and the Malay Archipelago. And until about 200 years ago it lived in England and ate the acorns and beech-nuts of those forests.

For thousands of years the wild boar was hunted in England. During the Roman occupation of the island, the legionnaires hunted it enthusiastically, and today in the town of Ribchester you can still see a sculpture with a wild boar on one side of the stone and the motto of the Twentieth Legion on the other. The word "boar" appears in many English place names, like Boarshill in Oxfordshire, and such names as Eversham and Everley come from the Saxon word for "boar," *eofor*. And the famous English chronicler Holinshed, from whom Shakespeare took the plots of many of his plays, mentions wild boars. He said that boar-hunting was suitable for gentlemen because it was a "very dangerous exercise."

It is not known just when boars became extinct in England. But they seem to have been exterminated during the seventeenth century. James I is known to have hunted boars in Windsor Park, but the next monarch, Charles I, found they were so scarce that he had to import a number from France. These were released in the New Forest, the royal hunting preserve, but the English country people found them so formidable that they made every effort to get rid of them. After the civil wars of Cromwell, more attempts were made to bring back the boar to Britain; General Howe, of American Revolutionary War fame, was one who tried his hand. But it didn't work out; the people of Britain did not want such a dangerous animal in their forests. Today the European wild boar is found in Germany, Poland, Hungary, Belgium, Spain, and occasionally France. It also still survives in Russia and many Asian countries.

The European wild boar weighs between 50 and 350 kilograms (110 and 771 pounds). It has a large head, a short, bulky neck and a short, massive rump. The two upper canine teeth, which grow into tusks, have three edges and as they grow they bend upward and backward. The two lower, much sharper tusks have pointed tips and can be used as formidable weapons. In the females the tusks are weaker and are used for digging rather than fighting. But if she is threatened, the sow can use her tusks to good advantage. In winter the hogs grow a dense underfleece below their long, dark bristles. The coarse outer hairs are especially long on the neck and back, where they sometimes form a crest.

Food, Food Everywhere

The wild boar is the animal from which all our domestic breeds are descended, and Dr. Bernhard Grzimek, a well known authority on animal life, says the domestic pig can return to the wild more easily than most domestic animals. Perhaps one reason is that it will eat almost anything. It is not confined to certain kinds of grains and vegetation, as are horses or deer. Neither is it confined to a meat diet, as are cats and dogs. Wild boars are great rooters in the forest floor, where they dig up roots and tubers. They dine on nuts and many kinds of shrubs and weeds. But they also eat any meat they come across, from worms and grubs to birds' eggs and snakes; even carrion. They have also been known to catch grasshoppers and mice and to dig up clams.

The wild boar is a massive, tough animal that can weigh more than 700 pounds. It survives winter conditions well with the help of an underfleece that grows in as the weather becomes cold.

A story that illustrates the resourcefulness and adaptive eating habits of *Sus scrofa* was reported in 1952. It concerns a female pig in Puerto Rico that had acquired, nobody knows how, the habit of going fishing in the ocean. Twice a day she went into the sea, always at the same shallow spot, and rooted about, with the water up to her ears, probing for fish. When she caught one she would pull it out and eat it, and then duck back to search for more. She spent about four hours a day in this activity and often caught as much as 30 pounds of fish. Sometimes even a baby shark was snared, and fascinated fishermen and children often gave her some of their catch. She became so famous that she was known as La Pescadora ("The Fisherwoman") and her owner swore she would never go to the slaughterhouse. She seemed to realize that she was something special and refused to fraternize with the other pigs.

This wide range of eating habits has enabled pigs to live in many habitats, from dense forests to arid deserts, from boggy marshes to mountainous terrain. But unfortunately for them, as human agriculture has spread they have come in contact with gardens and planted fields. These are very attractive to wild boars, which come out to forage at dusk and find a garden or potato field an excellent place for rooting. Naturally this rouses the anger of the farmer and leads to the extermination of the pigs.

Foresters also are inclined to dislike wild boars. By rooting up the soil and eating the nuts they may change the type of woodland that they live in. Oak forests may in time turn into woods of birch or firs. But the pigs' depredations are not all bad, for as this activity loosens the soil, it may bury seeds; and the animals also eat substantial amounts of tree parasites, such as the larvae of cockchafers and sawflies, and the caterpillars of some destructive moths. The problem of wild boars in European forests is that most of their natural predators have been killed off, so that there is no control of their numbers. Farther east, in Russia, there are still wolves which may serve to keep the population in check. And in the Asian habitat, tigers, leopards, and lynxes still prey on the pigs. Of course, in many so-called wildlife preserves, the human hunter is all too happy to step in and act the role of predator.

Courtship and Boar Families

Since they spend so much time rooting about in the underbrush, wild boars do not rely primarily on their eyesight, and their sight is not very keen. But their senses of smell and hearing are extremely good, and a hunter must be expert to creep up on them successfully. While male wild boars are usually solitary, the females and their offspring are gregarious, and go about in groups of six to ten or even more individuals. Sometimes these groups consist of one sow and her offspring. Or there may be two or more sows with their litters, making a much larger group.

When the males become mature, they leave the herd for their solitary way of life, but they return when a sow comes in season. At such times there is

The wild boar, Sus scrofa, *can be seen in some zoos. It is no beauty, but it is an interesting animal to study.*

competition among the males for as many females as possible, and a returning mature male will drive off the younger males in the group. Then there will be vicious fights among the male boars, in which each contender tries to cut the other with his tusks.

Since the lower tusks are directly below the top ones, they keep sharp by rubbing against each other. When the males fight, they try to gore each other from below, and their bloody wounds leave grim traces on the ground or the snow. As a protection, the males have developed a kind of "shield," which grows just before the rutting season. On both sides of the chest, thick tissue develops that forms a rugged plate about two inches thick. It reaches from their shoulders as far back as the last ribs. This protection probably prevents undue mutual slaughter. Males try to acquire more than one female during the mating season. Usually an aggressive male will collect three sows for himself, but in some instances a boar has been known to win as many as eight.

Courtship among the wild boars has its special rituals. Once the male has rounded up his sows, he must persuade them to accept him. To do this he drives the sow in circles, at the same time poking her and rubbing her with his snout. He urinates often and makes odd, rhythmic, grunting noises. French scientists have discovered that this behavior induces her to stand still so that actual mating can take place. The zoologists made a tape recording of a boar's mating sounds and later played it back to a group of young females. They found that most of the sows then stood perfectly still, even allowing people to sit on their backs.

Wild boars are devoted mothers, and the sows will attack any intruder that threatens their young. The younger the piglets, the more aggressive the mother, and she will chase away all other animals, with the exception of another sow and offspring.

When the pregnant sow is about to give birth, she

leaves the group she has been living with and goes off to find a quiet, well hidden spot where she makes a nest, usually under thick vegetation. There she digs a large hollow which she lines with leaves and grasses for softness. She then scratches nearby vegetation into the hollow, walking back and forth over the material. She bites off other leaves and carries them from a distance. Sometimes she even brings branches to make a kind of roof. It is said that domestic pigs too sometimes do this, for piglets are very small when they are born, with hardly any hair, and they need protection against cold and rain.

The average litter for an older wild boar is five or six; young mothers have fewer. The infants stay in the nest for about a week, lying close together for warmth. The mother stays with them, and if she does leave for a short time she usually covers them with leaves or grass. When they get older they go out with the mother but return frequently to the den to rest. The little striped piglets stay close to their mother, and when she senses danger and gives an alarm signal, they all freeze. When nursing, the mother lies down on the ground and calls them with soft grunts. They gather in a row along her side and often fight among themselves for the best spot, thus establishing a kind of "suckling order." When they get older they often run after the sow, squeaking and butting at her side until she lies down to feed them.

Wild boar piglets stay not only with but sometimes on their mother as they romp about. The sow is always on guard against any possible threat to her young.

Only a few of a litter live to grow up. Many succumb to the cold and rain of spring storms or are eaten by predators or become fatally infested with parasites. Less than half the litter survives, an average of two young for each sow.

Boars of Our Own

While the wild boar has been exterminated in England and confined to small areas in most of Europe, it has surprisingly found a new home and habitat in the United States. No real pigs are native to the Americas. Instead, our fauna has a smaller, more distantly related animal, called the peccary. But early in this century an American businessman, who owned a large hunting preserve in the Smoky Mountains in North Carolina, thought it would be a good idea to import some European boars so that there would be a large game animal in his preserve. George Moore did business with a group of Englishmen, and when they came to this country to meet with him, they enjoyed good hunting on his preserve.

Fourteen young animals, weighing only about 50 pounds each, were brought over. They were brought from Germany, but the local farmers believed that they came from Russia, and they have been known as "Roosian boars" ever since. Moore imported other animals for his English friends to hunt, such as bison, elk, and black bears. The preserve was fenced with wire to keep these animals from straying, and a special enclosure was built for the boars. But the builders had no concept of the great strength of the wild boar and its dislike of confinement. In time they broke out of their enclosure and easily escaped past the outer wire fence.

All this was very annoying to the small farmers living in the area, for the wild boars drove off or killed their domestic boars and mated with their sows. The offspring of these crosses were much wilder than the farmers' domestic pigs and they were hard to fatten. They would not eat as much as did the real domestic hogs. Eventually most of the farmers were moved out of the area when it was made into a national park. The Great Smoky National Park now covers 512,000 acres, part of it in North Carolina and part in Tennessee. It has a variety of habitats, including great pine and hardwood forests, valleys crammed with such dense growths of laurel that they are known as "laurel hells," and high, grassy mountain slopes. All of it is attractive to the wild boars, which now number over 1200.

It looks as though the animal is here to stay. Biologists wishing to study a rather large animal in the wild can go to the Smokies, instead of making a costly trip to Africa. And such scientists are welcome in the national park, for it is important to know how the new species will affect the environment. Game wardens must watch for possible deterioration of the forest caused by their intense rooting. There are no predators to control their numbers, for the wild boar can stand up successfully to a bear or to a pack of dogs. Some hunting is allowed, and poaching takes place. And the park management sometimes live-traps individuals for study or for transport to other areas. Such wild pigs are given vaccination shots against the diseases that afflict domestic hogs.

There are free-ranging wild boars in Texas also, along with more than 30 other kinds of animals that originally came from abroad. Among these are deer, antelopes, and—surprisingly—giraffes. Some of these

This North Carolina wild boar was trapped in an area where boars were so numerous that they were a threat to crops. It is being released in a remote area where the wild-boar population is low. NORTH CAROLINA WILDLIFE RESOURCES COMMISSION

many "displaced" species live in refuges or on ranches, but others have escaped and now live in the wild.

The Story of "Grunt"

In Germany too the forest manager must make careful study of the wild boar herds in his area, for here also the predators have been killed off, and the forester must be sure that the boars do not destroy their habitat with their unrestricted rooting. An interesting picture of such activities and the animals involved has been given by Dr. Margaret Altmann, a scientist who earlier had specialized in moose and elk research at Jackson Hole, Wyoming. There had been complaints of boar depredations on potatoes and other field crops of western Germany, and there was some thought that the pig herds might have been augmented by animals from the neighboring Communist countries.

Altmann stayed with a forester's family while she was studying the pigs, and there she made the acquaintance of a remarkable sow. Her story illustrates not only the great intelligence of these animals, but also how easy it must have been for early human farmers to domesticate the species.

This sow, whom the foresters called *Grunze* (Grunt) had been picked up by a truck driver who was driving at night through the forest and saw the little piglet, apparently abandoned at the roadside. He gave it to the forester and it was raised by the family. When grown she was released into the forest behind the ranger's house, but she came back periodically and was always given a meal of potatoes and grain.

Although she lived mostly in the forest, Grunt had learned how to open doors in the ranger's buildings. At times she got into the milk house, where she raided the milk and cream pots, leaving something of a mess in her wake. One winter day she came into the yard and watched the rangers piling fresh straw and hay into a warm hayshed. When they were done she moved into the shed, made herself a nest there and in a few days gave birth to her first litter.

However, tragedy followed. One of the infants fell through the slats of the hayshed and landed in the dog kennel, where it was promptly killed by the dogs. Grunt was frantic. She bit at the slats of the shed until her mouth was bleeding, but she could not reach her baby to help it. So that same night, in spite of a heavy snowstorm, she took her remaining offspring away into the forest. Everyone at the ranger station felt that the little pigs must perish. But three days later Grunt brought them back, re-established herself in the hayshed and raised her babies without more trouble.

Unfortunately Grunt did not fare as well. One day in spring she opened a shed door and got into a bag of grain that was stored there. It was poisoned grain for rat control; within two hours poor Grunt was dead. Altmann says that her piglets continued to visit the ranger station, and while she was making her study they would follow her into the forest. They loved to have their backs scratched, and if she scratched one, the others would come running, jealously demanding the same attention.

3 · A Pig with a Beard

There are three other species in the Sus genus besides *Sus scrofa*, the wild boar, and they all live in eastern Asia. The wild boar, which has the widest range of all pigs, is often found in the same areas, living in close proximity to its cousins. The bearded pig, *Sus barbatus*, lives in southeastern Asia, in the Malay peninsula and nearby islands. It is a large animal but not nearly as heavy as the European wild boar. These pigs have long legs and a distinctive, hairy beard on the cheeks, not seen in most other wild pigs. In one strain, the beard is curly and even covers the ridge of the nose. They have warts between the eyes and the teeth and also under the eyes, and their body skin is gray or sometimes pinkish gray. The skin is quite visible, since most of the hair is confined to the bearded face. Males are larger than females, and the tails are very long and flattened at the end, with a large tassel.

Bearded pigs prefer to live in tropical rain forests

or mangrove jungles. Their food is typical of that of most pigs: fruits, roots and shoots, and meat such as insects and grubs. However, as people continue to claim more of the jungles for farmland, the two habitats often coincide, and when the bearded pigs come upon plantings of yams and manioc, they find them very much to their taste and become a pest to the farmers.

In some parts of Borneo, the bearded pigs—the only wild pigs on that island—make regular migrations at certain times of the year. Hundreds of animals are seized, like lemmings, with the impulse to move elsewhere, and they journey along well trodden paths. Hardly stopping to eat, they rush on over all obstacles, swimming streams and climbing mountains. They are remarkable for their swimming ability and have been seen swimming across ocean inlets. One was lassoed from a ship in the middle of Sandakan Bay, where it was trying to swim to a point some three miles away. When swimming, they stay low in the water with only the snout and top of the head showing.

Eating Rice, Then Being Eaten

In describing a mass migration of the bearded pigs, E. Banks wrote that along their route "rice crops are utterly destroyed, but they do not deviate. . . . Silent, not quarrelsome, almost furtive, intent on something, looking round but little, they push on undeterred by waiting natives, who club and spear them at river crossings until weary of pork."

The human settlements in Borneo are unusual in that all the people who live in the coastal regions are Mohammedans, and for them pork is taboo. So pigs are safe from hunters while they stay near the coast. But the people living in the interior of the island, the Dajaks, have no such inhibitions. And when the pigs migrate toward the interior they are slaughtered by the hundreds. They are waylaid on their migratory paths and those that try to escape by swimming are speared and their bodies washed downstream to waiting tribespeople. In 1956-57, so many pigs were killed that there were not enough containers to hold the lard and even boats were used as receptacles. In 1954 the slaughter was so great that the rivers were blocked and the water developed a bad taste. This almost brought about a war between the Dajaks and the Mohammedans on the coast. The latter said that their water was being poisoned. In some parts of the island, where the pigs do not migrate but stay near the coast, they are free of this persecution.

Bearded pigs, like most of their relatives, live in large family groups, and sometimes they form a kind of symbiotic relationship with other species of animals. They are tolerant of the crowned wood partridge and allow the birds to pick up worms that they have just turned up with their rooting. They also let them pick ticks off their skin. The birds are helpful to the pigs also by sounding an alarm at the first sign of danger. Then the pigs run for cover. Bearded pigs also make a practice of following along on the ground when a group of monkeys such as macaques, or gibbons (which are apes) are moving through the higher branches of the trees. When the monkeys or apes drop the fruits they are eating, the pigs are right there to collect them.

Like most of the swine family, bearded pigs make special nesting places each day, where they can rest after eating. But when a female is about to give birth, which happens once a year, she leaves the group and builds a much more elaborate nest. Usually this is done in the jungle, where she amasses a large mound of leaves, ferns, and branches of trees. She digs a burrow into the mound and in this safe, cosy hiding place she gives birth. Usually there are four to eight young, but on Borneo the sows are apt to produce only two or three to a litter. The little striped piglets stay with their mother for about a year.

Borneo is an excellent habitat for the bearded pigs, as long as they stay away from the tribes in the interior. There are few large predatory animals for them to fear. No leopards or tigers exist there and the only remaining big cat, the clouded leopard, is being hunted to extinction. And humans, the greatest and most feared of predators, here leave the pigs alone because of religious scruples.

The Johore Migration

On the Malay Peninsula the bearded pigs also migrate, turning up in Johore, the southernmost part, in the month of June. By November they have disappeared from that region and moved elsewhere. Their wavelike migrations make well trodden tracks, inviting to hunters, who wait for them along these paths. Here the pigs like to get into the tapioca fields and to eat the kernels of the oil palm and rubber-plant seeds. They are not as secretive as their cousins, the wild boars, which are also native to the peninsula. They do not hide in swamps during daylight hours, but may start feeding in early afternoon. And if they do go to rest, it is in high jungle rather than swampy areas. Thus they are easily hunted with dogs.

When they first arrive in Johore, the sows and their young are said to be undisturbed by men and guns, but the males are more wary and keep at a distance. When chased by dogs, they do not turn and fight, as do the European wild boars, but run as fast as they can through dense jungle, thus losing their pursuers. When they have experienced much hunting, the pigs usually take to feeding at night. The hunters then go after them with torches. And while the European boars will run if a light is turned on them, the bearded pigs are inclined to freeze in their tracks, offering the hunter a good target.

During their sojourn in Johore, young pigs have not been observed with the herds, so it seems that their breeding season must be spent elsewhere. After November the animals disappear from the southern districts of the peninsula and are not seen again till the following June.

J. A. Hislop has told of an unusual experience with the pigs. On a hot day in 1945 he and five companions were carrying heavy loads down a steep and difficult decline when they heard a loud roaring and squealing, which they thought must come from a herd of elephants. Although realizing the danger from elephants, they were unable to alter their course, and suddenly they found themselves in the middle of a huge herd of bearded pigs. Dozens of the great hairy creatures rushed past them, making a tremendous uproar but paying little attention to the men. A couple of large boars paused to stare and grunt and some actually brushed against them as they ran past. But they were all too intent on getting wherever they were going to be distracted. And the men, loaded down with their burdens, were happy to see them go.

Bearded pigs are not often seen in zoos. But in a zoo in Halle, East Germany, they recently had two females. These were crossbred with a European wild boar.

Several offspring resulted, but the scientists were unable to continue the line, for when these hybrids were mated among themselves, all their litters were born dead or died soon afterward. This, according to the distinguished zoologist Erna Mohr, "does not suggest a very close relationship between the bearded pig and the European wild boar." It would seem to be somewhat like the relationship between the horse and the donkey, which can produce the mule, but mules can produce no further generations.

4 · The Javan Pig, Rugged Pioneer

On the islands off southeastern Asia there is a third species of wild hog, popularly known as the Javan pig, *Sus verrucosus*. The three species overlap in their range, often being found simultaneously in the same general area. Thus the European wild boar, with the widest range of all pigs, inhabits Sumatra, Java, the Lesser Sundas, East Indonesia, and New Guinea. The bearded pig is found on Sumatra and Borneo, while the Javan pig lives on Java, Borneo, Sumatra, and the Celebes.

The most unusual feature of the Javan pig is its very long head. The pigs weigh up to 150 kilograms (about 330 pounds) and the faces of the boars are decorated with "warts" or lumps on each side of the face. The sows and young pigs do not have these facial features.

On Java, *Sus verrucosus* is less likely to be seen than the more common wild boar, *Sus scrofa*. The boar is more adaptable to people and not as easily frightened away from towns and villages. The Javan pig prefers to live in rugged, unsettled areas. It ranges from sea level, where it often comes to search for food along the shore, to the highest mountains. When they are seen from a distance, it is often difficult to tell one species from the other, but the Javan pig has a lighter-colored underbelly and a reddish-brown row of bristles down the back; *Sus scrofa* is entirely black. The Javan pig also has more curve to its back and bigger ears. When it is alarmed, it makes a shrill whistling noise, whereas wild boars grunt.

Like all the pig family, the Javan pig is a general feeder, eating the fruits of wild figs and various palm trees, digging up turtle eggs and finding washed-up coconuts along the beaches, even attacking chickens and goats if it is given the opportunity. When it roots around fruit trees and in planted fields it often does more damage than by directly eating crops.

Since much of the population of Java is Moham-medan, pigs are not hunted for food. But they have been systematically persecuted and destroyed for decades because of their depradations to agriculture, and it is remarkable that there is still a large pig popu-lation on the island. However, the animals are very adaptable, with a high survival rate. Preferring to feed in the daytime, they quickly switch to eating at dusk or even at night if they have been attacked and

LEONARD LEE RUE III

These wild pigs, like all members of the pig family, survive by being able to eat anything that comes along. The ground here is thoroughly disturbed by the pig habit of rooting in the soil for part of their food—a trait that can be helpful in keeping soil cultivated but usually does more harm than good around fruit trees and vegetable plantings.

frightened. Of all the wild animals on Java, they are considered the least endangered.

Protecting and Observing

In recent years a sanctuary and game reserve has been established at Udjung Kulon, and the naturalist A. Hoogerwerf has described his observations of the Javan pig. He says that he never watched a pig building a nest, but has found many of these throughout the reserve. The nests are likely to be bigger in the dry months than in the wet and are seldom built in open country, though occasionally he found them in cultivated fields. They are usually built in forests with dense undergrowth.

The vegetation nearby is bitten off, dragged to the nest and piled up, thus creating an open area around the animal's home. The nests vary in size, probably according to the ages of the sows that build them, and look much like a heap of garden rubbish. The largest one measured by Hoogerwerf was three meters (about ten feet) across and 75 centimeters (about 30 inches) high. At the base there is an opening, not easily seen and seemingly much too small for a pig to enter. Hoogerwerf surmises that the sow simply pushes her way inside and lets the nest material fall back on top of her. The hollow within the nest is lined with leaves and here the sow gives birth to her piglets, and then returns periodically to suckle them. There are usually four to eight piglets in a litter and they are not striped, as is usual with most of the pig family. Some observers say that very dim stripes can be seen in the proper light, but if so, they quickly fade.

Although Hoogerwerf never found any piglets inside the nests he examined, he was told by hunters of finding infants in such nests, varying from very young to about three weeks old. In cases where a sow and young were disturbed in a nest, the sow usually ran off, leaving the piglets, which scattered or cowered deeper into the nest. Even the squeals of an infant that has been picked up does not bring the mother back to help, but it is presumed that she returns after the hunter has gone and reassembles her brood with soft grunting calls. Since Hoogerwerf never observed piglets much younger than a month following their mother, he believes that the sows keep them well hidden in the nests until they are fairly large.

Boars are thought to build nests also, but not as elaborate and only for sleeping and resting purposes of the moment. The reserve has many streams and water holes where pigs, as well as creatures like the rhinoceros, can make wallows. The Javan pig likes to wallow in mud as much as any pig, and the little piglets will follow their mother into a wallow. Such holes must always contain a degree of mud. The observer never saw pigs bathing in clear water. A mud

A good many of the wild pigs of the world are found in Asia, particularly in the southeastern part of it around the Malayan peninsula. The Javan pig lives not only in Java, but also in Sumatra, Borneo, and the Celebes.

coating serves wild pigs (and various other mammals) as an effective protection against biting insects.

Getting Along with Others

Like the bearded pigs in Borneo, the Javan pigs are on good terms with other animals of the wild. They can be seen feeding in the same area with deer and wild cattle, and a variety of birds often follow the herds about. Peafowl, egrets, storks, and crows may hop about between the pigs, snapping up grasshoppers and other insects that the herds scare up. Some species of birds even ride on the backs of the pigs, picking off any parasites they can find. As on Borneo, the birds act as alarm sentinels for the pigs, signaling the approach of any enemy. Usually the pigs do not run at the first cry of a bird. But if they have been sufficiently alarmed by hunters and if the cattle stampede, the pigs will dash for cover without pausing to look back.

The Javan pig seems to be a much more timid animal than is the European wild boar. Even in this farthest area of its range, *Sus scrofa* will often turn and fight, and the sow will defend her young. But *Sus verrucosus* is inclined to run and scatter first and think about the young later. With hunters pursuing them on every hand, perhaps this tactic has a good survival value.

5 · The Pigmy Porker

The smallest member of the pig family is the pigmy hog, *Sus salvanius*, which lives in the southern foothills of the Himalayan Mountains, in such places as Utter Pradesh, Nepal, Sikkim, Bhutan, and Assam. It looks like a minature or toy pig, standing 25 to 30 centimeters high (about 10 to 12 inches) and measuring 50 to 65 centimeters (about 20 to 25 inches) from head to rump. It stands slightly higher in the rear, and the sides of the body are flattened. Some have white hair on the cheeks and a crest of bristles along the back. They have small ears and a ratlike tail and the body hair is sparse, coarse, and long. The color is black or rusty brown.

These "miniature" animals were first discovered in 1847. In the early years of the present century no pigmy hogs were sighted in the wild, and it was feared they might have become extinct. However, in the early 1970s they were rediscovered in Assam, when a

HORMEL INSTITUTE, UNIVERSITY OF MINNESOTA
Besides the pigmy hog Sus salvanius *there are small-sized pigs in various parts of the world. The specially bred laboratory pig on the right weighs only 13 kilograms (about 30 pounds), as contrasted with the barnyard pig on the left, which weighs about 81 kilograms, or some 180 pounds. One of the pigs it was bred from is found in Guam, an island northeast of Borneo. This photograph is a composite of two separate pictures, because the miniature laboratory pig was disease-free and could not be safely brought near the barnyard pig.*

forest fire near a tea plantation flushed a herd out of the undergrowth. The workers on the plantation began to kill the animals as a tasty addition to their food supply, but two avid conservationists who were in charge at the plantation halted this slaughter by offering to buy live pigs at a much higher price than would have been paid for dead ones. Consequently most of the herd was captured and the continuation of the species assured.

It now seems probable that the pigmy hog was never in danger of extinction. They are so small and keep so well hidden in the jungle underbrush and grasses that people are seldom aware of their presence. The males do not live alone, as in most species of wild pigs, but stay with the herds and protect the young and the females. If they are flushed out of the undergrowth by fire, the little pigs show great agility in escaping. Usually the herds are small, consisting of only five or six animals, but occasionally they may number 15 to 20. The adults defend themselves energetically, using their sharp tusks to good effect. Elephants are said to panic if the pigs are found in their way, for the small creatures can cause painful gashes on the feet and legs of the giants.

Originally it was thought that the pigmy hogs were nocturnal animals, but now it appears that they merely stay hidden during the torrid noonday periods. They come out to feed in early morning and late afternoon. Like all pigs, their diet is varied. They dig up roots and bulbs, but also eat eggs, insects, and small reptiles. In captivity they are very fond of rice and corn on the cob, and will carry a cob about, nibbling at it, till all nutrition is gone.

Close-Knit Groups

Watching these captive pigs, observers have learned that, like their larger relatives, they build extensive nests, piling up the grass to make a structure with both entrance and exit holes, and usually well hidden. They are very gregarious creatures, staying close together when feeding, and piling up on one another when going to sleep. While herds today are quite small, in 1891 they were reported to assemble in droves of 50.

Only when she is about to give birth does the female pigmy hog leave the herd and make a well concealed nest for herself. Pigmy sows have three pairs of teats—only half the number of most pig species. Their litters number from three to four young. The piglets are striped but observers say that the markings are faint and hard to see.

Unlike most pigs, these animals do not take to marshy ground but prefer dry areas of the jungle, covered with scrub and thatch plants, such as bamboo. During the rainy season such plants grow as high as 12 feet, but then wither and shrink to about five feet as the rains cease in the dry season. When the thatch becomes too waterlogged during the monsoons, the little pigs retreat to the more forested regions of the foothills.

Since the rediscovery of the pigmy hog, strenuous efforts have been made to ensure the survival of the species. The captured animals have been sent to several zoos, where they are being carefully tended and encouraged to breed. And in their wild home, the Assam Valley Wildlife Society has fenced off a square mile of the best habitat as a sanctuary for them. It is hoped that the fence will keep out wandering cattle and trespassing humans who might want to farm the land or kill the pigs. But there is one problem not faced by the usual wildlife sanctuary: elephants. Wild elephants do feed in the area and the great beasts would have no trouble in pushing down the fence. The society believes it will need frequent repairs, which may prove to be a costly item in its budget.

6 · Bushpigs, the Garden Raiders

The most widely distributed of all the African wild pigs, the bushpig, is found everywhere south of the Sahara desert, as well as on the island of Madagascar. Because of this wide distribution there is a great difference in the appearance, color, size, and other details of bushpigs from different regions of the continent. Nevertheless they are basically the same animal and scientists have now agreed that they all belong to the same species, *Potamochoerus porcus*.

Bushpigs are up to 80 centimeters (about 31 inches) in height and up to 150 centimeters (about 59 inches) long. Their tusks are not very long but are extremely sharp, since the upper ones are always grinding against ⸱e lowers. They have long, pointed ears and a tassel at the end of the tail. In some localities they are very colorful. Their body color varies from reddish brown to black, sometimes mixed with white or yellow hairs. Occasionally there is an almost white pig or one

65

mottled black, white and brown. The Cameroon bushpig is brightly colored, with a white mane along the
back and long hairs hanging from the pointed ears.
When displaying for a female or another male, the
boars arch their backs so that the white mane stands
up like a crest, and they extend their ears and tails so
that the long hairs become conspicuous. Like most
wild pigs, they have ugly "warts" on the face, though
these are partially hidden by the long hairs of the
beard.

These pigs tend to be nocturnal, hiding in the forest
during the day and coming out to find food at dusk or
at night. They are partial to animal food and in captivity will eat ground meat, dead chickens, or fish.
But they are also fond of plants—especially those
raised in gardens, as has been discovered by the
farmers of South Africa. Here, where the predatory
animals such as leopards have been killed off, the
bushpigs have greatly increased their numbers and
become a pest to the local farmers. They make great
depredations on the peanut crop, as well as on pine-
apples, grapes, corn, and even watermelons. They
can smell carrion from a distance and sometimes attack small barnyard animals, digging under even
"jackal-proof" fences.

The victimized farmers have gone to great lengths
to protect themselves against the pigs, but poison has
proved ineffective, since the pigs can smell the bait

and refuse to eat it. Hunting with dogs is also of little use, as the pigs fight off the dogs, often killing them. This is a typical example of what happens when people kill off the predators of a region, allowing the prey animals to increase unnaturally. Odd methods of dealing with the situation have been developed. Some farmers recommend setting out a bowl of beer and waiting for the pigs to get drunk, when they can safely be killed with a hammer. Others have tried the ruse of taking a domestic pig up into a tree and making it squeal. When the wild pigs come to this cry of distress, the farmers shoot them.

"Plowing" the Ground

Bushpigs are great rooters, digging up the ground with their tusks and snouts. In captivity, according to Dr. Grzimek, they make their pens look like the craters on the moon. During the day they hide in dense thickets or reed beds, where they make burrows and tunnels. They are gregarious and usually seen in groups of from four to 20 individuals. Sometimes a half-grown boar will accompany an old boar, a habit also observed in the European wild boar. The French refer to this younger boar as the "page" of the older one.

As these animals are nocturnal and seldom observed in the wild, most records of their behavior

The bushpig, Potamochoerus porcus, *is found in zoos through-out the world. This one was photographed in open sunlight, but ordinarily this species hides in the semidarkness of dense forests during daylight hours.*

come from zoos. There are usually between two and eight piglets in a litter and as usual the infants are striped. Their average life span is 13 to 14 years, although that may be stretched to 20 years with an unusual individual.

As with the other two species of African pigs, the bushpigs do not seem to fight each other with their tusks, thus cutting down the chance of severe injuries.

Instead, they have pushing matches, forehead to forehead. Even a male and female in the Frankfort Zoo indulged in such pushing as a kind of play-fight. With their foreheads pressed together and their snouts crossed "like crossed swords," the two animals would push back and forth, the long hairs on their ears waving and their tails swishing like whips. As long as they were young, these bouts were all in good fun. But when they got old, the male became cross and greedy and would chase his mate away from the food trough, so that their keeper had to take special measures to be sure that she got enough to eat.

C. T. Astley Maberly, a naturalist well experienced with African wildlife, admits the damage done by the bushpigs to agriculture. But where the paths of pigs and farmers do not cross, he believes that the animals may have a beneficial effect. In the forests and the uncultivated bush they perform a kind of natural cultivation, turning up the soil, spreading seeds about, and destroying injurious insects. This rooting action also hastens the decomposition of leaves and tree branches, improving the soil and helping it to retain moisture.

Alarm Signals

Maberly often observed the bushpigs that came to his farm and marveled how their white and red markings blended with the dappled sunlight on the leaves. The family groups would be in charge of a big old boar, who was alert to any sign of danger. If he caught a movement from the watcher, he would snort, his tufted ears would shoot up and the whole group of pigs would freeze. If the boar was further alarmed, he would make for the forest, grunting and gnashing his teeth, while the crest of bristles along his spine stood up—making him look, as Maberly put it, like a huge porcupine. The rest of the herd nearly always rushed after him.

If any pigs failed to heed these warnings, they were vigorously disciplined by the old boar. The naturalist described one occasion when he was watching his cornfield at night and became so absorbed in the antics of the pigs that he gave up all thought of shooting at them. One young pig was so busy enjoying an ear of corn that he failed to notice that the group had become alarmed and had slunk away into the forest. When he suddenly found himself alone, he dashed after his family, and Maberly heard his high-pitched squeaks and squeals coming from the woods, where the old male was apparently dealing out punishment.

7 · A Colonel's Giant

Although it is the largest of the swine family, the giant forest pig of Africa was not discovered until 1904. At that time one was shot by Colonel Meinertzhagen, a British officer in Kenya. He was honored by having the species named after him, which is why it has the complicated scientific name of *Hylochoerus meinertzhageni.*

The giant forest pig stands up to 110 centimeters (about three and a half feet) tall and weighs up to 250 kilograms (over 550 pounds). This makes the animal a giant among swine, but it would seem a dwarf if compared with some of its prehistoric ancestors. Africa, which once was home to 11 genera of pigs, now has only three: the giant forest pig, the bushpig, and the warthog. Some of the fossil pigs were as large as hippopotamuses or rhinoceroses, and the giant forest pig would seem to be the last of the titans.

Forest pigs are colored brownish black, with a few white hairs on their long, ungainly faces. There are also small tufts of hair on the ears, and the tail sports a tassel. The tail is carried pointing upward as the pig runs. Like all the African pigs, these pigs often have ugly growths and swellings on the face. The eminent zoologist Dr. Erna Mohr describes them as looking like a sponge growing on a tree trunk. The boars also have a saucerlike hollow in the middle of the forehead and both sexes have very large snout discs.

The giant forest pig discovered by Colonel Meinertzhagen is a jungle dweller of great wariness; probably this specimen feels quite exposed in the open yard of a zoo.

NEW YORK ZOOLOGICAL SOCIETY

Secretive Ways

The reason why the species remained unknown until this century is probably that they have secretive ways and that they live in the dense jungles of central Africa. They are very shy and rarely venture far from the protection of the forest. While they may occasionally come out onto the grassy plains to feed, they retreat to their forest strongholds at the slightest danger, and seldom are a threat to farmers' crops. They are believed to go about in small family groups, including a male, a female, and several young.

Such a group has its own territory, large enough that it can move around and still keep to its home range. They make tunnels and paths through the densest jungle, with a number of dens scattered about, so that they can occupy a different den every day. Since each family keeps to its own territory, there is not much fighting among males. When they fight, they do so by placing their foreheads together and pushing. Perhaps this explains the uses of the strange disclike depression on the foreheads of the males.

A distinguished African explorer of the early twentieth century, Carl E. Akeley, observed a group of forest hogs on the slopes of Mount Kenya. He reported that they had piled up regular haycocks, to three feet in height and eight to 10 feet in diameter, but he could not guess what use these were put to. Today, with our modern observations of pig behavior, we can guess that they were for sleeping or resting nests, or possibly the nests of a sow that was about to farrow (give birth). Females of the forest pig are extremely protective and aggressive; few of the piglets are captured by predators. Zoo records show that the litters are from six to eight young and the gestation period 125 days.

The Matter of Diet

Strangely, these pigs of the dense African forests are not much given to rooting and digging up the forest floor, as do most pigs. Instead, they prefer to eat fresh greens, such as grass, young sprouts and fruit; and they are very fond of sweet-potato tops. They also visit salt licks to eat the salty earth. The usual pig fare of roots and bulbs is outside their diet. For this reason the species has never lived long in zoos, where they were apt to get ordinary hog food instead of fresh greens. More recently, in the Frankfurt Zoo, where the proper diet was available, a male lived for three years and a female for over two.

Like most pigs, the giant forest hogs are gregarious and devoted to each other. A report from the Uganda Game Department tells of a boar that had been wounded by a spear and was partially paralyzed in the hind legs. He was limping badly and four of his family were close around him, trying to help him out of a mud hole and making a great noise about it. This sort of mutual-aid behavior has also been observed in other species of pigs.

8 · The Warthog:
Monstrosity of the Plains

The African pig that is probably most often seen by tourists is the warthog, *Phacochoerus aethiopicus*. One reason is that it is a daytime animal, whereas most of its relatives are nocturnal in feeding habits. Also, it runs about on the great African plains, along with the many other hoofed creatures and various predators, where it is often glimpsed by busloads of tourists bent on seeing African wildlife.

Warthogs are slate- or clay-colored and grow to be up to 190 centimeters (some six feet) long and up to 85 centimeters (nearly three feet) high at the shoulder. The body is barrel-shaped and the head is remarkably long, with the face flattened and shaped like a spade. The eyes are set high and far back. On this grotesque face, in addition to the two pairs of curving tusks, grow two sets of large skin protuberances, usu-

76

*This sparsely haired male warthog almost suggests a species of
cattle as it stands drinking at a pond. Note the indented tusks
and the four "warts" above them.*

ally referred to as warts. Tusks and warts are bigger in the males than in the females. The animals have little hair on their bodies, aside from a kind of mane on the neck and along the back. There is also hair around the face. A tassel on the end of the tail stands up perkily when they run.

Helpful Adaptations

We may wonder how nature could have developed an animal with such a bizarre appearance, but when we consider some of its habits we can see how well they and various bodily features match each other. As warthogs live in the more open habitats of Africa, the scrub and thornbush, thin forest and grassy plains, their food is chiefly grasses. But as they have fairly long legs and short necks, they have developed the habit of going down on their front knees when feeding. Warthogs eat the young, green shoots of grass, biting them off close to the earth. In these grazing habits they are in competition with the many other hoofed animals of their habitat: antelopes, bison, zebras, and such. In the rainy season there is plenty for all, but during a drought they must search diligently for every last bit of green. In these circumstances, the warthogs search carefully under the thornbushes and other prickly growths to find the last little shoots that may be sheltered there. They get down on their knees and push their heads through the sharp spikes. It might be thought that their eyes and faces would suffer, but here is where their large facial warts serve them well, protecting both the eyes and cheeks. It is said that after a drought, the warts of the warthog are as full of thornbush spines as a pincushion is of pins.

While kneeling on its front knees and feeding, the warthog is in danger of attack from any of the predators of the African wild: the lions, hyenas, leopards, and wild dogs. But the high position of their eyes helps them to keep an alert watch; and once a warthog has wheeled to face its enemy, few predators will continue the attack, for the two sets of tusks are terrifying weapons.

The lumpy "warts" on a warthog have a useful function when the animal feeds. SAN DIEGO ZOO

Going Below

The warthog has another defense against predators: unlike other members of the pig family, it takes refuge in burrows deep underground. But it seldom has to make its own burrows, because its body is almost the same size and shape as that of another burrowing mammal, the aardvark. This animal, also called earth pig or ant bear, is no relation to the warthog. It is an insect-eater and lives on termites. While its body is roughly the same size as the warthog's, its head is long and thin, with a pointed snout and very long tongue. It digs its burrows all over the warthog's territory and the enterprising pigs are quick to adapt them to their own uses.

Aardvark burrows are a shelter from any sudden danger. The young pigs run straight into them head first, but adult warthogs have developed the habit of going in rear first, thus presenting their sharp tusks to any enemy that might think of following them down the hole. When a family of warthogs senses danger (for warthogs live in families, like all pigs) the little ones go down the hole first and a big male is usually the last to go in, backing in so that his big head and tusks completely block the entrance.

Only occasionally does this habit backfire. One observer tells of watching some animals on the African plain. When he got too close to a group of hyenas, one of them went down a hole while the rest of the group ran away. He was about to go over and inspect the hole when a nervous warthog came running by. The unfortunate animal had not seen the hyena go into the hole and, anxious to get away from the human observer, he quickly turned tail toward the hole and backed in. The results were what might have been expected. The next instant a squealing warthog erupted from the hole and dashed off with blood streaming from his rear end.

Mother and Piglets

Warthogs also use the aardvark burrows as nurseries. Here the young have much better protection from bad weather and the night cold than do their relatives that make nests of leaves and grass aboveground. The mothers do not need to carry leaves and grass into the burrows. Here their infants are safe and the sows can leave them for long periods during the day while they forage aboveground, returning now and then to suckle the young. When they are about a week old, the piglets begin to follow their mother outside for short trips. But they frequently go back to the den. As they get bigger, the den is used only at night.

The young pigs stay with their mother for about

A mother warthog with her young. Notice how high the eyes of the adult are on the head, a feature that helps protect warthogs during feeding.

a year. They are solid-colored, without the stripes usually seen in young pigs, and until they are half grown are covered with reddish hair. Aardvark dens often have several rooms. One such abandoned burrow, created practically in a termite nest (where the aardvark had settled close to its food supply), had once sheltered piglets in one room while another was being used by some bats.

Warthog sows have only four teats, so that it has been presumed that litters can be no larger than four. But more recently it has been found that sometimes there are six little piglets. Dr. Grzimek, reporting for the Frankfurt Zoo, says that litters average between two and seven and that the warthog's life span is from 10 to 12 years, with some individuals living even longer.

Fighting and Feeding

Warthogs seldom fight among themselves. However, when the female comes in season, there may be competition among the males in the area. In one account of a typical case, a lone male approached a family group. The male heading the group allowed his family to move a certain distance away and then turned to confront the newcomer. He made a ritual display in front of him by trotting in a stiff-legged, jerky manner and turning sidewise, which showed the mane standing erect along his back, his tensely arched body, and pricked-up ears. The head and tail were held horizontally. The stranger seemed to pay no attention, but when the family male rushed at him, he lunged back. They met head on and a pushing contest ensued, tusks meeting tusks and snout shoving snout. After a few minutes of pushing, the two broke off and went back to feeding.

These bouts of fighting and feeding continued for about 40 minutes, after which the new male seemed to be tiring. While the struggle seemed to be about equal, it was conducted in silence except for a few grunts from each side. But as the interloper began to tire, he went down on his front knees in a defensive position. His ears were flattened, his mane lay flat, his tail curled upward; and with each lunge from the old male, the new one let out a highly pitched squeal. Eventually the stranger took advantage of a feeding break to run away. The old male chased him for a short distance and then returned to his family.

Strangely, the old male showed no inclination to fight with a young male that was a member of his group, even though the youngster was displaying to the sow. However, the female paid no attention to the young male's advances, and it was only after the older male had defeated the newcomer and then approached his sow that she accepted him. The boar displayed in much the same way as he had done to the invading stranger, by turning sidewise to her and raising his mane. Then he moved up behind her and rested his chin on her hindquarters. At this, the female raised her tail and backed into him and mating was achieved.

While warthogs seldom hurt each other when fighting, confining their activities to these pushing contests, they can be very ferocious and courageous when confronted by enemies. They can run at 30 miles an hour, but they will also turn quickly to fight, and other animals recognize the danger of their tusks. One observer reported seeing a sow and piglet being chased by a leopard. All at once the sow turned and charged the leopard, which gave up the chase and ran away. On another occasion some elephants were seen to be pursuing a warthog and trumpeting in anger. But when the pig stopped running and charged the big tuskers, they gave up the attack and backed away in apparent surprise.

9 · Balloonlike Babirusa

One of the strangest and most peculiar-looking species of all the pigs lives in southeastern Asia on the Celebes and nearby islands. They can weigh up to 100 kilograms (about 20 pounds), have small, pointed heads, an arched back, and long, slender legs. The body is barrel-shaped and hairless, and the gray or brownish skin is sometimes smooth but often very wrinkled. The tail is short and without a tassel. This pig's scientific name is *Babirussa babyrussa.*

This pig lacks the extraordinary "warts" or protuberances that seem to disfigure many of the pig family, but it makes up for that with its bizarre tusks. Especially in the male, these grow in a remarkable way. The tusks in the upper jaw erupt through the broader part of the snout and grow straight upward, eventually curving back toward the face and eyes. Since this gives a vague appearance of an antlered animal, the Malayan natives call them *babi* ("pig") *rusa* ("deer").

This accounts for both their scientific and popular names. The Germans call them *hirscheber,* meaning "deer boar."

Most Curious Tusks

There is a belief among the natives that the creatures can hang by their tusks from branches in the forest. This is hardly possible, even if the pigs were so inclined and sufficiently acrobatic, for the tusks are quite brittle and break easily. Georgia B. Dittoe, who cared for a pair of babirusas in the San Diego Zoo, says that a keeper once seized an old babirusa by his tusk only to have it crumble in his hand. And Ms. Dittoe herself once shut a cage door too quickly, so that it hit the male babirusa in the face. It was only a light blow, but four inches of the big tusk were broken off. For some time the animal was disfigured by having uneven tusks, but the broken tusk grew faster than the unbroken one and eventually caught up with it. Perhaps it is just as well that these great, curving tusks break easily, for it is said that they can grow in an almost complete circle, and if they push against the pig's head, can grow right through the skull and into the brain, in time killing the unfortunate beast. The tusks in the lower jaw are more normal and grow straight up before they, too, make a backward curve.

The peculiar tusks of the babirusa can hardly be listed as weapons. Some scientists think they are more likely defensive devices, used for warding off blows. Even in the wild they seem to be easily damaged, and most of the skulls in museum collections have broken or damaged tusks. In fact, these fancy tusks seem to be more of a hindrance than a help and probably even get in the way of feeding. Babirusas do not root in the ground as do other pigs, but dig insects out of rotting trees and enjoy eating leaves and fruits. They communicate with grunts and squeaks, and chatter with their teeth when excited.

A Peaceful, Primitive Pig

The babirusa is only distantly related to the other species of pigs. It is considered to be a primitive form. But whatever its physical characteristics, its behavior is very piglike. The animals live in small family groups, occasionally staying by themselves. They like reedy thickets and swampy forests where they can wallow. They are good swimmers and easily cross rivers and wide arms of the sea. Villagers who have kept them as pets say that they tame easily. But as they are also often hunted for food, there is some fear that the species is endangered. As with all the Asian pigs, the continued clearing of the forests to make farmlands is wiping out their habitats.

In spite of its formidable array of tusks, the babirusa is not an aggressive animal. Some scientists suggest a reason for this. They argue that mammals use a display of teeth as a defensive threat toward a possible enemy—thus a dog will snarl befort it bites. In fact, it raises its lip and shows its teeth on the side where the adversary stands. Monkeys and many other animals also behave in this manner. And the bigger the threatening weapon that is displayed, the less likelihood that the animal will have to use it.

The babirusa's tusks are fragile and one or more is rather often found to be broken off. Far back in its evolutionary history there may have been babirusas with strong tusks, but those with fragile ones were more likely to survive a full lifetime.

SAN DIEGO ZOO

Thus the greatest fighters among the pigs are the little peccaries, whose tusks show hardly at all, but can be used to very good effect. The next most aggressive are the European wild boars, which have comparatively short tusks. The African pigs, with their longer, more impressive tusks, do not use them for fighting with each other, but engage in pushing contests instead. And the babirusa, with the most imposing tusks of all, hardly seems to know how to fight. Perhaps the nonuse of the babirusa's tusks accounts for the general weakness and uselessness of these parts, and even for the erosion of the animal's aggressive instincts—though in such matters it's hard to say just which is cause and which is effect.

The female babirusa has much smaller tusks than the male, but she seems to have no trouble in holding her own against her more formidable mate. Ms. Dittoe says that in the case of one she observed, she did this vocally. If the boar pushed her out of the way at the feeding trough, the sow would let out such ear-splitting shrieks that he soon gave way. Even when she managed to seize some delicacy and carry it away to a corner of the cage, she would go on screaming.

The babirusa sow is deficient in nursing equipment. She has only two nipples, and so cannot raise more than two piglets in a litter. The infants do not have any stripes.

Hard To Find

Babirusas have not been studied extensively in the wild and are not often seen in zoos. Those at the San Diego Zoo are the elite among the pigs there, having cost more than any of its other swine. This is probably because of the difficulties in obtaining them from their home in the Celebes. There are strict quarantine laws against importing all hoofed animals into the United States, because of the fear of bringing in the dreaded foot-and-mouth disease. Moreover, in recent years the Pacific nations, noting the rapid depletion of their wildlife, have imposed drastic laws against such exports. However, babirusas do well in zoos and have reproduced in several establishments. One kept in the New York Zoological Park is described as being good-natured, liking to have his back scratched. During the winter months he would become bored with indoor life, and used to let himself out of his winter quarters by lifting the door latch with his snout. In captivity, babirusas live an average of ten years. And one female even reached the advanced age of 24.

10 · Peccaries, the Yes-and-No Pigs

There are no true swine in the fauna of the New World. We do have the little peccaries, whose genus name is Tayassu, and because they are piglike in certain ways they are included in this book. But they are far more distantly related to the true pigs than their appearance would indicate. Their small size would seem to make them comparable to the pigmy hog, and their bristly coat and trunklike snout do give them a piglike appearance. In such important matters as teeth, stomach, and feet, however, they are closer to that other group of even-toed, hoofed mammals, the ruminants.

Their upper tusks do not grow out and upward, as with the pigs, but point straight down, as with predatory animals. These are strong, three-edged daggers, constantly being sharpened by scraping against the lower teeth. While peccaries cannot be said to have definite multiple stomachs, like the ruminants, they do have three clearly marked glandular regions of the

These three collared peccaries came from Arizona. Peccaries are rather small; they weigh up to about 31 kilograms (some 68 pounds). As the one on the right is "demonstrating," their upper tusks grow straight down.

stomach and in the front part are two sausagelike cul-de-sacs. The arrangement of the bones of their feet is also more like those of the ruminants than of the pig family. And while they have the usual four toes on the forefeet (the extra two toes do not touch the ground) there are only three on the hind feet.

Another odd thing about the peccaries, not found among swine, is a gland at the rear of the back. It lies just under the skin, hidden by the long bristles. The animal can cause the bristles to flare apart, exposing that area of skin and emitting an oily secretion which has a strong, musky smell. This gland is just above the spot where the tail should join the body, but peccaries have no visible tails. Their rudimentary tails are hidden inside.

Whitish Bands

Peccaries stand about 55 centimeters (some 21 inches) at the shoulder and are about twice that long. When adult they weigh up to 31 kilograms. The adults are blackish brown, and the bristles sometimes give them a pepper-and-salt appearance. They have no underfleece, which would hardly be needed in their warm-to-hot environment. The bristles are thicker on the back and shoulders and can be erected as an aggressive threat if the animals are alarmed.

There are two main species of peccaries, each with a number of subspecies. The collared peccary (*Tayassu tajacu*) has the much wider range, being found from southern Texas, New Mexico, and Arizona through Mexico, Central America, and much of South America. The white-lipped peccary (*T. albirostris*) does not come as far north as the United States and is confined chiefly to Central and South America. The white-lipped is the larger of the two and is reported to be more aggressive. Each has its own distinctive markings. In the collared peccary, it is a band of yellowish-white hair running in a semicircle around the shoulders. There is also a black stripe running down the

The white-lipped peccary, Tayassu albirostris, *has a band of whitish hair that gives it its name. Peccaries weigh up to 31 kilograms (about 68 pounds).*

length of the back. The white-lipped peccary has a whitish band on the lower jaw below the eye. It has coarser, thinner hair and the musky odor from its gland is much stronger.

Odors for Identity

The piglets of *T. albirostris* are the more colorful, being a rusty red. They keep this coloring for the first year, a fact confusing to early observers, who thought they were a different species. Both species share the same habitat in much of their range, and are able to interbreed successfully. This is probably prevented in the wild by the difference in the glandular smells. Scientists have argued that the scent gland must be used for sexual attraction, bringing the males and female together at the proper time. But it seems also to have other uses, such as marking of territory. For the animals have been seen to rub against trees, bushes, and rocks and thus spread their scent around. It goes even further than this, for the pigs rub up against each other. When resting, they often lie close together, head to rump, so that each individual can obtain the other's scent. In this way the whole group, or herd, comes to have a distinctive smell, and it is doubtful if an animal of the other species, with a quite different odor, would be welcomed as a sexual partner.

Occasionally one pecccary in a zoo's herd will be rejected by the rest of the group and continually chased away. The unfortunate animal must eat and sleep alone and in time probably loses the group smell, so it is then even less likely to be taken back into the herd. These animals are usually sold to another zoo, where it is hoped they may start their own group or be accepted by the animals already there.

While peccaries are different from the Old World pigs in their physical structure, they are very similar in diet and behavior. They eat a variety of grasses, leaves, and fruit such as wild figs, according to what can be found in their habitat. They also eat roots and cacti, which are prevalent over much of their range. The prickly-pear cactus is a favorite. As the animals grow older, their rather poor sight is often made even poorer by the development of scar tissue on the eye. This is probably caused by the spines of the cacti it has been feeding on, for as these little pigs have never evolved the protective "warts" of the African hogs, they have no such shields against thorns.

Like the Old World pigs, our peccaries also like some meat in their diet, and in addition to grubs and adult insects, are known to catch and eat small snakes and other reptiles. Like the true pigs, they are believed to be immune to snake venom.

Retreat and Attack

Peccaries also resemble the pigs of Europe and Africa in their behavior patterns. While both species are cautious and alert, vanishing like shadows at the slightest sound of danger, they are also aggressive and courageous. They have developed the tactic of group attack to a fine art. The Old World pigs will usually run while one old boar, or perhaps the sow, stays to fight off the enemy; but the peccaries all rush together to the attack. So, although they are much smaller than their relatives on the other side of the world, the combined attack is more terrifying. The native predators, which include the jaguar, puma, and coyote, will seldom attack a herd of peccaries. They may try to get a piglet that has been left alone, or pick off the last of a long file of traveling adults. But they know well the effect of an angry group of peccaries rushing to the attack.

There are many tales throughout our Southwest and Mexico of hunters and photographers who were treed by a band of peccaries and had to spend a lengthy and lonely time in an uncomfortable and perhaps precarious perch. Some scientists tend to ascribe such adventures to the white-lipped peccary, which is bigger and more aggressive. They note that the victim is unlikely to make a good identification in the heat of the moment. And at least one terrifying pig charge turned out on analysis to be a case of cornered pigs trying to escape. But such tales have given all peccaries a reputation of sorts, and some ranchers in those areas make sure to be properly armed when they approach a group of pigs.

Dr. Frank M. Chapman, who spent many years doing field work at the science station on Barro Colorado Island in the Canal Zone, tells of his experiences with the white-lipped peccary. He says that they are usually nocturnal, whereas the collared peccary prefers daytime. Thus he was quite used to seeing the latter species around the station, where they were seldom troublesome. But, although he was anxious to make the acquaintance of the larger animals, it was only after five years, when there was a drought that caused a food shortage, that the white-lipped peccary appeared around the station.

Dr. Chapman was pleased to see a group in the clearing outside his living quarters, but it became less pleasant when the boar tried to keep him from going in his door. His assistant, Miguel, was with him, carrying his usual machete; by waving the weapon and shouting, he was able to chase the boar away so that Dr. Chapman could enter. But when the scientist wanted to come out, Miguel was no longer around and the peccaries were again occupying the area in front of his door and prepared to defend it. Dr. Chapman finally threw an empty bottle at the boar, hitting him on the nose. The pig squealed and jumped back, but then went to investigate the "strange phenomenon." He had seemed to be more surprised than hurt, but when he smelled the bottle, he jumped back so quickly that he knocked over the sow that had come up behind him. All the peccaries fled into the forest. As the bottle had held only water, Dr. Chapman believes it was his human smell that frightened the pigs away.

A Keeper Up a Tree

Dr. Chapman believes that the collared peccary is not nearly as aggressive as the white-lipped. However, the small herd of collared peccaries at the San Diego Zoo once dug out of their pen in a remote corner of the zoo and went on an exploratory tour. The keeper of the reptiles was on his way home through the zoo and noticed the rambling animals. He decided to herd them back to their enclosure, but the peccaries did not want to go. It ended with their chasing the keeper, who had to take refuge up a prickly rose arbor, where he was effectively treed by the charging animals until they lost interest and wandered away.

Eventually the pigs were all herded back to their pen, but when they were counted, it was found that two young boars were missing. They turned up the next day, having spent the time wandering near their enclosure. But when they were put back into the pen, after only 24 hours of separation, they were viciously attacked by one of the old boars and quite badly injured. It seems likely that the common herd scent had worn off in that time and that they were no longer recognized as belonging to the group.

This young collared peccary, shown with its mother, could be a fine pet—but only during the period before it reaches adulthood. SAN DIEGO ZOO

Pets and Herds

Young peccaries are especially appealing and often make charming pets, once they realize they will be treated kindly. But when they grow up they are unreliable and may attack their human friends. One bite from their dagger-sharp teeth can inflict serious wounds. A number of such grown-up pets have been given to zoos by disillusioned owners.

However, we must remember that most of these reports are of captive peccaries, and animals often behave differently in the wild than in captivity. Within a pen there is always a limit to how far an animal can run from a threat. Dr. William J. Bigler has reported on observations made on a population of wild peccaries in Arizona. There were 13 herds in the study area, totaling 106 animals, a third of which were juveniles. Eleven of the animals were immobilized with capture guns and color-marked. From this it was learned that one or two individuals were always straying from herd to herd, apparently without danger. This is rather at odds with reports of individuals being attacked and driven from captive groups.

The peccaries also seemed to be friendly and good-tempered with other species of animals in their area, a behavior pattern also noted in their relatives, the swine. They fed contentedly close to range cattle or deer. In fact, William H. Carr has told of a pet peccary at a ranch that had a close friendship with a mule deer.

The herds studied by Dr. Bigler each occupied a territory of from about one to three square miles. In winter the rains brought more vegetation and the pigs were well fed. In summer they spent the hot part of the day resting in caves. Though they are usually day-feeding animals, in the warm seasons they fed at sunrise or in the evening. When the temperature began to rise, they would leave the valleys where paloverde and mesquite shrubs were still green, and proceed in single file along well trodden trails up the sides of the canyon to caves they selected. At the cave mouth the leading boar would stand aside while the herd entered, one after another. Then he would follow them in. Inside, the pigs dug shallow depressions with their hoofs. There they huddled together in groups of three or four, with the young in the middle. When the sun began to set and the lower canyons were shaded, the peccaries would go back down the trails, always in single file, to find their feeding areas in the cool of the evening.

Bigler says that the young are born from June to August, which contradicts some reports that they reproduce at any season of the year. Females may mate with several males, but there is seldom any fighting among the boars. Twins are usually born, but sometimes three or four unstriped infants may be in the litter. Farrowing takes place in a cave or a hollow log. The sow has four pairs of nipples, but apparently only the two in the rear produce milk. This observation is doubtless based on captive animals. The mother peccary nurses her young while standing up; this is quite different from the true pigs, among which the mother always lies down. The milk supply is small and the young must drink often. There is a report from the Zurich Zoo of two infants that nursed not only from their mother but also from another sow that seemed to produce milk without having given birth.

Peccaries do not have the instinct of true pigs to make elaborate nests of vegetation. Instead they find shelter in caves or hollow logs, and they dig depressions in the ground with their feet. There is a story from Gerald Durrell's zoo on the island of Jersey of what happened when their peccaries were once accidentally shut out of the sleeping-quarters portion of their enclosure at night. In the morning it was found that the herd had dug up an area in the corner of their enclosure and built a mud mound around themselves. They had all slept facing outward, with their only infant in the middle.

Like their Old World relatives, peccaries are good swimmers. When fighting, they do not slash with their tusks, as do swine, but they can do plenty of damage by just biting. If they are angry or alarmed, they threaten with a kind of rattling noise, made by gnashing the teeth together very fast. They are quite long-lived animals, according to zoo records. The average life span is 20 years, but one peccary in the New York Zoological Park reached the age of 25.

Hunted Hard

The popular Spanish name for the white-lipped peccary is *puerco del monte* ("mountain pig") and the collared peccary is called javelina; either may be called a musk hog. During the 1930s the little animals were all but exterminated in the United States. Hunters pursued them with guns, dogs, and horses. Apparently they were considered good eating by the local people and their skins could be made into gloves and belts. Sometimes they were shot just "for fun" or to feed the dogs. More recently, hunting regulations have been passed and sanctuaries established, and their numbers are again on the increase. For the time, at least, we will still have peccaries within our borders. But there seems to be scant protection for the animals in Mexico and South America. Dr. Grzimek notes that in 1965 alone the town of Iquitos, Peru, exported 129,000 skins of collared peccaries and 30,000 skins of the white-lipped species.

It is startling to contemplate the differences between the pigs and the peccaries. Their point of separation lies far back in geologic time—an estimated forty million years. But while much has changed in their physical makeup, their basic character and behavior are amazingly the same. Both strains are omnivorous and gregarious, intelligent and courageous. These aspects would seem to be more enduring than the form of a foot or the nature of a tooth.

11 · Pigs in Laboratories

Throughout the long history of human civilization, extending for thousands of years into the past, the pig has been perhaps the most useful domestic animal—though hardly appreciated in that light. It has fed us more bountifully and with less work on our part. Its hide and its fat have found many uses for humans. Now it seems that it is going to do even more. It is going to help save lives.

It has long been said that the pig is remarkably like human beings in many of its physical aspects. This fact was recognized 500 years ago by the great Italian painter and experimenter Leonardo da Vinci, who studied the cyclic motions of the pig's heart. Much later, in the eighteenth century, the great British medical investigator John Hunter stated that the pig was the most useful of all animals for scientific study. This fact was also recognized in Germany about the same time, when the Margrave of Baden Dierlach (one of the small principalities) suffered what seemed to be a heart attack. His doctors agreed that a poultice should be applied over his heart, but they could not agree on the exact location of that organ. So at the command of the Margrave, a pig was dissected in front of him and the position of the pig's heart was taken to indicate just where the Margrave's heart must lie. While doctors did not know much about anatomy in those days, they were correct in assuming that the pig's heart is located similarly to that of a human.

Hysterical Whoppers

In modern times, the great Russian physiologist Ivan Pavlov at first used pigs for his experiments. But when a pig was put up on the examining table, it began to squirm and squeal, letting out piercing shrieks, which made work impossible. Pavlov concluded that pigs were too hysterical for use in the laboratory, and discarded them in favor of dogs. With dogs he made the well-known conditioning experiments for which he became famous.

Pigs were also found to be unsuitable for laboratory work because they grow to be so big. Adult pigs may weigh from 800 to 1500 pounds, and at that size they are quite unmanageable. Even if the pig behaves well, just lifting it on and off the table is a formidable task.

Both these pigs are six-month-old males. The one on the right is a miniature laboratory pig weighing only 28 kilograms, or about 62 pounds, as against the weight of 83 kilograms (about 185 pounds) for the farm-type Yorkshire on the left. Such "minipigs" are used for testing drugs and researching many other medical questions in laboratories today.

And pigs don't always behave the way we want them to. If an 800-pound pig wants to do something different, few humans can stop it and they may be badly hurt if they try. While few domestic pigs live to reach a weight of 1500 pounds—they are slaughtered for food long before that—in laboratory experiments it is often necessary for the animal to live out its life for researchers to determine the results of an experiment.

A Special Midget

Since Pavlov's day, a great deal has been learned about the raising and handling of pigs, and in recent years breeders have developed several special strains of pigmy pigs that grow to weigh no more than 150 to 200 pounds. At this weight they are easily managed in the laboratory, and their size is comparable to that of humans. For instance, a dose of medicine that would be correct for a pigmy pig would probably have a similar effect on a person.

Scientists have found these small pigs (sometimes called "minipigs") to be so useful for laboratory experimentation—much more so than the usual dogs, rats, or rabbits—that great efforts have been made to breed them, both here and in such countries as Britain and Germany. Some of the first work done in this country was at the University of Minnesota's Hormel Institute, where the breeders used five strains of small hogs—four from the United States and one from the Island of Guam. They succeeded in producing a pig one-third the size of an ordinary hog. Similar work has been done by the Pitman-Moore Company of Indiana and at the Battelle Northwest Laboratories in

Richland, Washington. Various strains of small pigs have been used to produce even smaller pigs. White and almost hairless strains have also been developed.

Complications in a Lab

Raising pigs for laboratory use is more complicated than merely raising them for food. Lab pigs must be carefully protected against the many diseases they—as well as humans—are prone to. These include cholera (against which they may be vaccinated), viral pneumonia, brucellosis, dysentery, and others. To assure that the pigs stay free of these infections, their pens must be as far as possible from any swine farms and on land that has never before supported pigs. The workers who care for them must be careful to stay away from outside swine—or from any other animals —that might carry any of the swine diseases. And to enter the lab pens, they must go through a disinfection area. They must always wash their hands and wear protective clothing while caring for the pigs, and their boots must be dipped in a special 5 per cent solution of disinfectant before they go into the pens.

There is also the problem of feed. All feed must come from a farm where pigs are not raised and be mixed under careful supervision. And there is the problem of the trucks that bring the feed, for such vehicles often are driven into swine pens. So it is better for the lab to have its own truck. All outside vehicles and persons not connected with the lab are kept away from the area where the experimental pigs are being raised.

Most laboratories provide their pigs with small wooden frame houses eight by eight feet, with an outside pen of approximately 49 by 28 feet. Heat lamps assure the proper temperature for the piglets, and sawdust is used for their bedding rather than straw, in which infants might get tangled and thus killed by the sow when she lies down. A high fence surrounds the entire area, to keep pigs in and unwanted visitors out. However, it has been found impossible to keep out such visitors as wild rabbits and birds.

Humanlike and Not So Human

While it is remarkable how similar pigs are to humans in many ways, there are still a number of differences, which must be taken into account by the experimenter. Because pigs have less hair than many mammals, it is often assumed that their skin is the same as ours; and, in fact, their rather hairless skin makes them ideal for studying the problems of and cures for skin diseases.

But the pig's skin is really quite different from that of humans. Whereas our skin is rich in blood vessels and glands, the porcine skin is just the reverse. Humans sweat through their skin, but a pig cannot. This is why the pig needs water of some sort in which to wallow. If pigs are denied water in very hot weather, they will urinate and then roll in their urine in an effort to cool and dampen their skins.

Pigs grow faster than humans, and they have a much more acute sense of smell. Sows have a higher cholesterol level than boars, while in people the situation is just the opposite.

In spite of these differences, pigs are proving to be very useful tools in the study of the many ills that trouble humans. Many of our diseases, such as ulcers, diabetes, heart disease, and cancer, are contracted by pigs also. And the new miniature breeds are much hardier than the monkeys previously used in many of these studies. They are also less expensive and more easily obtained than our closer relatives, the primates, and have better dispositions. As one veterinarian put it, they had yet to lose a pig caretaker, while quite a few such workers had been injured by monkeys.

Pigs, Liquor, and Food

One of the most interesting problems being researched with pigs is a study of alcoholism. In one experiment, the pigs are given several dishes to drink from. One has 5 per cent alcohol and water. Another has 10 per cent alcohol and water, and a third con-

*An enormous variety of research goes on all the time in govern-
ment, university, and institution laboratories, in which thousands
of animals of many kinds help produce important information.
The miniature pigs that have been specially bred for laboratory
work are a great advance, for the physiology of pigs is much
like that of humans, and they are subject to many human
ailments.*

tains plain water. The 15 two-to-three-year-old pigs in this experiment almost always choose to drink alcohol. By early afternoon they are all lethargic and inclined to go to sleep. If they walk around, their gait is unsteady. A younger group of pigs is being given 5 ounces of alcohol a day in water, a cola drink, or orange juice. The youngsters like the orange juice best. Such laboratory tests are showing that some of the pigs have liver problems.

Another line of research concerns teeth. Pigs' teeth, it seems, are much like human teeth and many of our future dental "miracles" are being tried out on the pigmy hogs. Pig teeth are slightly larger than human teeth, but they are the same types: molars and cutting teeth. Also, the animals begin with a set of baby teeth, just as we do, and gradually lose them as the permanent teeth come in. This gives dental scientists a good opportunity to study many of the problems of children's teeth. They have also tried out experimental methods of implanting new teeth in the jaw. In one such case, after the tooth had been implanted, they found the pig chewing on stones. No doubt, if a newly implanted tooth could withstand this kind of wear, it could do a good job for humans.

Nutrition is another important area in which minipigs can be of help. In some experiments, the importance of protein in the diet has been demonstrated. Young pigs that were given only 4 per cent protein in their food did not gain as much weight as those receiving a diet of 16 per cent. It was found that their organs, such as liver, kidneys, ovaries and heart, had shrunk. The amount of mineral in their bones also decreased. Furthermore, their antibody response—the ability to fight off disease—diminished. These changes are similar to those found in human children who have been raised on a protein-poor diet, as happens in many parts of the world.

A Highly Important Danger: Radiation

People working in the nuclear industries are especially anxious to know just how much radiation can be tolerated in certain circumstances. How much is safe and how much is not? And what can be done to help a person who has been accidentally exposed? As Dr. Leo K. Bustad has pointed out, new uses for nuclear energy are constantly being developed, such as small, portable power generators, for use both on earth and in space. It is very important to know how safe such devices are, in case their radioactive fuels should accidentally release dangerous radioactive dusts and gases, as happened in Middletown, Pennsylvania, in the spring of 1979.

These experiments often concern strontium 90, which is also a hazard of nuclear fallout from such sources as the testing of atomic bombs. Strontium 90 in the past has descended upon pastures where cattle were feeding and has been detected in milk that would normally be consumed by people. With these many new sources of radiation appearing in our environment, it is important to know what is safe and what is not, as well as what the long-range effects may be. Tests on humans cannot answer some of these questions until several generations have passed, but in pigs, with a life span of about 15 years, the answers can be found much more quickly.

It was found that pigs that received a nonkilling dose of radiation developed considerable resistance to later larger doses. In a study on the effects of radiation on fertility and genetics, it was found that male pigs, subjected to a certain amount of radiation on their genitals, could still produce offspring, although the number of sperms they produced had been reduced by about 20 per cent. More than 15,000 infant pigs have been sired by these irradiated males, and in the case of one breed, Duroc, an unusual result appeared: the litters were slightly larger than normal.

Hearts, Drugs, and Burns

Probably the most important research that can be done with pigs will turn out to be in diseases of the heart and circulation. The animals are likely to develop these conditions and thus they are ideal for studying them and trying to develop a cure. Pigs are also used for testing the many drugs developed for treating human heart disease. In the case of certain drugs, dicumarol and heparin, used to thin the blood and prevent clotting, it was found that a too-small dose was worse than no drugs at all: it actually had a clotting effect. This experiment showed how important it is to find and prescribe the proper dosage.

Modern medicine is constantly improving and inventing new operations to save the lives of severely ill patients, but new techniques must first be tried out and evaluated in the laboratory. In this the minipig plays an important role. And pigs have for a long time furnished the ingredients of some of our most important and sometimes life-saving drugs: insulin for diabetes, heparin for preventing blood clots, ACTH for arthritis, leukemia, and many other diseases, and thyroxine for sluggish thyroids.

There are two other life-saving gifts from the pig as well. One is the use of pigskin in severe burn cases. Where human skin has been completely burned away, pigskin, used as a bandage, relieves the agony of the patient. It can easily be peeled off, as it clings without sticking.

And for some 60,000 victims of heart disease, new heart valves have been fashioned from those of pigs. While doctors do not know how long such implanted valves will last, they have not had a "catastrophic failure" during the ten years they have been in use. And without them, those patients would probably all be dead.

The "Lowly" Pig Is Smart

Pigs are so intelligent that they are good subjects for behavioral studies, and now that the minipigs have been bred for laboratory use, they are appearing more often in such experimental work. They are also good-tempered and cooperative. If the pigs are well treated, they show a good response to their handlers, and it is quite safe to go into their pens in a way that might amaze some farmers. However, some researchers say that in picking experimental animals from a litter, it is advisable to select the piglets that come most readily to the experimenter. Such pigs prove to be more ready to explore their surroundings, and they seem to have the least fear of human beings.

In one experiment the pigs were taught to operate a panel type of switch by pushing against a white spot on the panel with their noses. This turned on an infrared heat lamp, and the pigs soon learned to heat up their pen in this way when they were subjected to cold. Pigs that were used to being handled and were at ease in their surroundings often learned this trick within a few minutes. Pigs that had not been as carefully selected sometimes took a little longer, but it was

Minipigs are used for behavioral experiments too. This one is learning to put on a switch by pushing against a white spot on a panel. Pigs brought up in a relaxed way with much human handling tended to learn it more quickly.

possible to draw their attention to the switch by fastening a brightly colored tape to it with one end protruding into the cage. As the animal chewed on the tape, it soon learned to connect the panel with "more heat." In some of the experiments the pig was given a choice of temperatures ranging from 23° to

37° Celsius (73° to 99° Fahrenheit). It was found that they usually preferred a temperature of 30°C (86°F).

If they are handled considerately, the pigs seem to enjoy doing such experiments, and in cases in which the animal must stand in a harness or a restraining compartment, they will trot right in and wait to be hooked up and for the experiment to begin. One researcher has said, "Once they know it [the task] they really look forward to performing every day." One such performance was for a pig to trot into a box and push a panel with its nose. A door than opened electronically and the animal was allowed to depart. The purpose was to check its performance of this little task before and after it received radiation, such as is given to people in treatment for cancer.

All in all, it seems that we owe a great deal to pigs— for food and quite a number of other benefits over the millennia. And that debt is likely to grow in the future, as pigs help us to understand ourselves better and to conquer some of the more fearsome ills that still plague us.

Suggested Reading

Books

J. Gunnar Anderson, *Children of the Yellow Earth* (The M.I.T. Press, Cambridge, Mass., 1973)

Bernhard Grzimek, *Grzimek's Animal Life Encyclopedia*, vol. 13, Mammals (Van Nostrand Reinhold, N.Y., 1972)

William Hedgepeth, *The Hog Book* (Doubleday, N.Y., 1978)

Perry Jones, *The European Wild Boar in North Carolina* (pamphlet available from Div. of Game, N.C. Wildlife Resources Comm., Raleigh, N.C. 27611; rev. ed., 1972)

L. E. Mount and D. L. Ingram, *The Pig as a Laboratory Animal* (Academic Press, London and N.Y., 1971)

Charles Towne and Edward Wentworth, *Pigs from Cave to Corn Belt* (University of Oklahoma Press, Norman, 1950)

Ernest P. Walker, *Mammals of the World* (Johns Hopkins University Press, Baltimore, 1964)

F. E. Zeuner, *A History of Domesticated Animals* (Harper and Row, N.Y., 1963)

Magazine Articles

Margaret Altmann, "Grunt, My Wild Boar," *Animal Kingdom* (N. Y. Zoological Society), Feb. 1957

Anon., "Fishing Pig," *Life*, June 23, 1952

Vernon Bailey, "Peccaries—The Native Pigs of America," *National Nature News* (Washington, D.C.), Oct. 17, 1938

Belle J. Benchley, "This Little Pig," *Zoonooz* (San Diego Zoo), Sept. 1939

William J. Bigler, "Seasonal Movements and Activity Patterns of the Collared Peccary," *Journal of Mammalogy*, Nov. 1974

Nicholas H. Booth *et al*, "Swine Production for Biomedical Research," *Laboratory Animal Care* (Amer. Assn for Animal Science, Joliet, Ill.), June 1966

Kent Britt, "The Joy of Pigs," *National Geographic*, Sept. 1978

Maurice Burton, "Warthog: Most Grotesque of Mammals," *Illustrated London News*, May 18, 1963

Leo K. Bustad, "Pigs in the Laboratory," *Scientific American*, June 1966

William H. Carr, "Wild Pigs of the Desert," *Natural History*, Oct. 1946

Frank M. Chapman, "White-Lipped Peccary," *Natural History*, Dec. 1936

Georgia B. Dittoe, "A Pig by Another Name," *Zoonooz* (San Diego Zoo), May 1945

Christopher Farmer, "Collared Peccary," *Report of Jersey Wildlife Preservation Trust* (Jersey Island, England), no. 7, 1970

Barbara Ford, "Pigmy Pigs," *Science Digest*, May 1972

John B. Holdsworth, "Peccaries," *National Wildlife*, Feb. 1969

Alan C. Jenkins, "The Wild Boar," *Animals* (London), Feb. 23, 1965

H. Lea Lawrence, "Wild Boar of the Appalachians," *Natural History*, Oct. 1969

Edward R. Ricciuti, "The Bizarre, Violent, Funny World of the Wild Pigs," *International Wildlife*, March-April 1979

C. David Simpson, "Observations on Courtship Behavior in Warthog," *Arnoldia* (Harvard University), Oct. 26, 1964

John Tessier-Yandell, "Rediscovery of the Pigmy Hog," *Animals* (London), Dec. 1971

Index